DISCOVERING
OLD NORFOLK

THE ROAD TO THE PAST

DISCOVERING
OLD NORFOLK

THROUGH THE PHOTOGRAPHS OF
TOM NOKES (1869–1943)

SUSAN WRIGHT

HALSGROVE

First published in Great Britain in 2011

Copyright © Susan Wright 2011

British Library Cataloguing-in-Publication Data
A CIP record for this title is available from the British Library

ISBN 978 0 85704 110 4

HALSGROVE
Halsgrove House,
Ryelands Business Park,
Bagley Road, Wellington, Somerset TA21 9PZ
Tel: 01823 653777   Fax: 01823 216796
email: sales@halsgrove.com

Part of the Halsgrove group of companies.
Information on all Halsgrove titles is available at: www.halsgrove.com

Printed and bound in the UK by the MPG Books Group

Contents

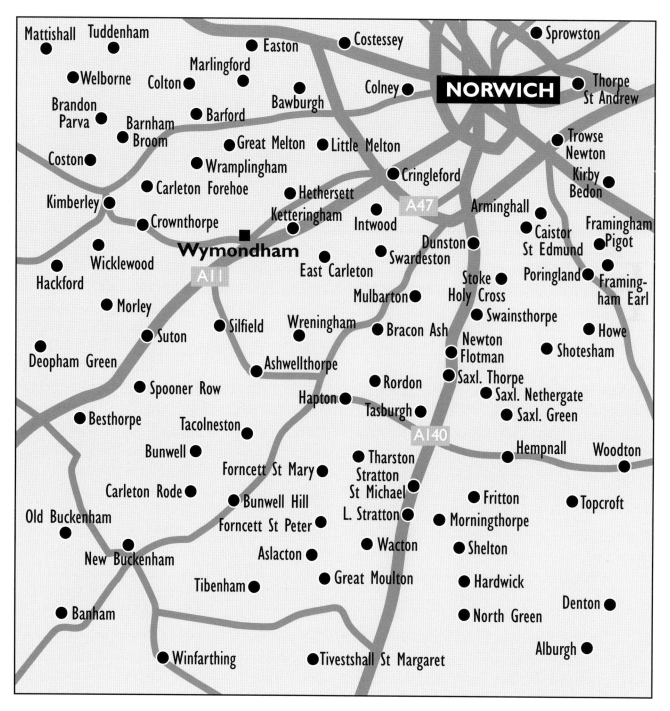

Map of South Norfolk.

Acknowledgements

FIRSTLY, MY sincere thanks to the family for their time and patience, Janice Barber, Jack, Hornsby and especially Shirley and the late Frank Jones for their excellent family photographs and access to Tom's notebook. Also thanks to Belinda and John Hornsby for their earlier research.

I should like to thank the following for their generous contributions:- Richard Bartram, John Betts, Sue Bird, Raymond Boileau, David Brake, Richard Fowle and the Wymondham Town Archive, Iris Frost, Pat Graham, Mary Guttridge, Brian Hardyman, the late David Marshall, Mary Parker, Bill Reekie and Hethersett Parish Council, Michael Signy, Colin Wilson, Jill Wright and Philip Yaxley.

A special thank you to Mary Standley for her time and kindness in allowing me free access to the wonderful Philip Standley collection.

Finally, this book would not have been possible without my husband, Tony, for his enthusiasm, encouragement, time and support. As I have no computer skills he has typed the manuscript, produced all the digital images, carried out online research and sent numerous e-mails on my behalf. A very big thank you.

Photograph Captions

Foreword

DESPITE HIS humble beginnings, my grandfather Tom Nokes had the tenacity, enterprise and skill to become at the beginning of the twentieth century a respected photographer. Cycling from Norwich to outlying villages south of the city, he created graphic legacies with his camera of those bygone years which ranged from momentous occasions such as the coronation celebrations of George V to rustic pictures of everyday life. Many of these photographs he transposed on to the postcards which are now so sought after by collectors. He was also a talented painter in oils and a wood carver. Unfortunately in the 1920s, with the advent of the Kodak Brownie and with no studio of his own, he could no longer make a living as a professional photographer and so became a painter and decorator.

I knew my grandfather in his later years. When I was a child of six, I remember him trundling a cart containing all his possessions around to our house in order to lodge there for a while. He was homeless. I can see him now – a tall, slim, upright gentleman with silver hair and a curled moustache – sitting erectly in our living room and thrilling me by blowing a succession of smoke rings into the air from his pipe. Then when mealtime came, he aroused my childish curiosity by remarking that he would like "bread and pull it" for tea!

Grandfather Nokes died in 1943 in obscurity – a forgotten man. And so it remained for nearly half a century. Then aficionados of early photographs began to recognize his originality and progressive style. Articles appeared in newspapers and magazines inspiring his great grandchildren, Belinda and John, to do further research. However, nobody has researched his life and work more assiduously than Sue Wright and I have been delighted to witness the development of this wonderful testament to the life and work of my grandfather.

Janice Barber (née Hornsby)

THE NOKES FAMILY TREE

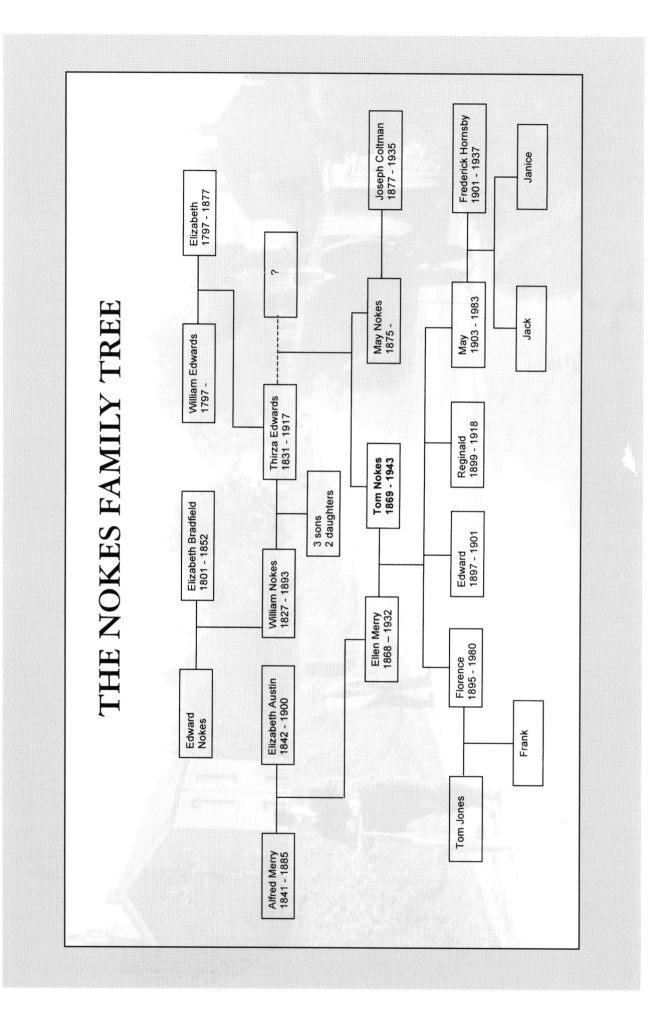

Tom Nokes – The Life of a Norfolk Photographer

TOM NOKES was a highly talented photographer, artist, self-taught carpenter and wood carver, painter and decorator. A slim, active sociable man, he and his attractive wife had two daughters and two sons. Local historians and postcard collectors are very familiar with his photographs but his personal life has remained in the shadows and he has appeared to be an enigma.

The photograph overleaf of a well-dressed, handsome and seemingly prosperous young man is one of the earliest images we have of Tom.

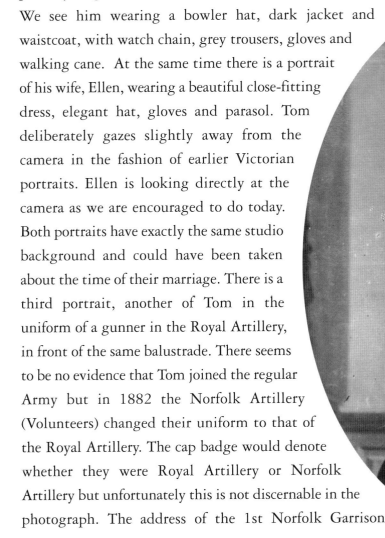

Studio portrait of Tom. F01

We see him wearing a bowler hat, dark jacket and waistcoat, with watch chain, grey trousers, gloves and walking cane. At the same time there is a portrait of his wife, Ellen, wearing a beautiful close-fitting dress, elegant hat, gloves and parasol. Tom deliberately gazes slightly away from the camera in the fashion of earlier Victorian portraits. Ellen is looking directly at the camera as we are encouraged to do today. Both portraits have exactly the same studio background and could have been taken about the time of their marriage. There is a third portrait, another of Tom in the uniform of a gunner in the Royal Artillery, in front of the same balustrade. There seems to be no evidence that Tom joined the regular Army but in 1882 the Norfolk Artillery (Volunteers) changed their uniform to that of the Royal Artillery. The cap badge would denote whether they were Royal Artillery or Norfolk Artillery but unfortunately this is not discernable in the photograph. The address of the 1st Norfolk Garrison

Artillery (Volunteers) was: Old Militia Barracks, All Saints' Green, a short
distance from his home, and it is probable that for a period of his young adult
life Tom joined and trained as a gunner in the Norfolk Artillery (Volunteers).
In the photograph he appears slim, fit and good looking.

The reality of Tom's life was very different from that conveyed by the
portraits. Tom's mother was Thirza Edwards who was born in Great Hockham,

Studio portrait of Ellen
probably taken about the time
of her marriage in 1895. F05

Norfolk, on 12 July 1830. Her father, William, was a licensed victualler. The family photographs we have of her show a rather prim and severe elderly lady. These photographs were taken in later life when she lived with the family at 9 Chester Street. Again, the photographs disguise the real person. It is said that she was high-spirited and found life in Hockham rather dull and decided to go and live in Norwich. There was some connection with the Lamb Inn and it is

*Portrait of Tom in uniform
with the same studio
background as F03 and F04.*
F04

possible that she worked there as a barmaid. Thirza married William Nokes in 1850.

In the 1861 census William was a billiard-room proprietor living at 15 Distillery Street with wife Thirza, three sons, William, Edward and Alfred, a daughter, Rosa, and a general servant. In the 1871 census Thirza was living at Eagle Street and was separated from her husband. It has been said that the separation was acrimonious and that this happened before 1871.

It appears that Thirza did not register Tom's birth and this could have been so that in later life he had outward respectability. He recorded in his notebook that he had been born on 25 February 1869. On his marriage certificate in 1895 his age is given as 25 and that his father is William Nokes. His death certificate, dated 30 December 1943, gives his age as 73. These ages are at variance with his own stated date of birth but this was not uncommon. On various census forms his place of birth is given as Norwich. Tom had a younger sister, May, and again there is no record of her birth, but Tom's notebook records that she was born on 5 May 1875. Her marriage Certificate states that her father was William Nokes, publican (deceased). The family maintain that Tom and May never discovered who their real father was.

Thirza remained separated from her husband, William. In 1868 and 1871 he was recorded as the proprietor of the Star Commercial Hotel, Haymarket, and in 1881 he was an hotel keeper

Portrait of Thirza Nokes with daughter May taken in front of a rustic porch in the back garden of 9 Chester Street. F06

Portrait of Thirza Nokes with daughter-in-law Ellen taken outside the back of 9 Chester Street. F07

The Lamb Inn, Norwich. The family says that Thirza worked here when she first came to Norwich. This is not a Nokes card. F15a

residing at 47 Haymarket, with a daughter, Jane, who was born about 1863. They had a housekeeper and three servants.

Tom and May's early years could have been difficult because of Thirza's separation: she had to work to support them. According to a story handed down within Tom's family his education was rather sketchy. He was given a few pence for school fees by his mother but decided to play truant on occasions and kept the money for himself. Clearly Tom became interested in photography at an early age; how was this interest stimulated? He was a boy from a humble background with little education but he managed to acquire an apprenticeship with Shrubsole of Norwich.

Portrait of Ellen in elegant clothes probably taken in the back garden of 9 Chester Street. F08

William Lewis Shrubsole was born in Kent in 1846. When he came to Norwich he soon established himself as a leading photographer. His patrons included HM the Queen, Their Royal Highnesses the Prince and Princess of Wales and Prince Albert Victor, as well as some of the landed gentry of Norfolk. In the 1879 *Kelly's Norfolk Directory* William Shrubsole was living at 1 Ely Place, Caernarvon Road, Norwich and in 1883 at 8 Connaught Road. It is recorded that in 1883 he had a studio in Davey Place and in 1888 two more studios, Exchange Street and Victoria Studio in St Stephen's Road. In 1898 he had a studio in Brigg Street.

The Boileau family archives have photographs taken by Shrubsole on their Ketteringham and Tacolneston estates between 1879 and 1898. We also know that Shrubsole photographed a wedding at Merton Hall in 1889. Nobody knows how long Tom was an apprentice but during that time he might well have assisted the photographer and been introduced to some of the landed gentry.

In 1891 Tom was living with his mother at 50 Rupert Street and was working as a photographic printer. In an article written by Philip Standley in

Norwich Lodge, Ketteringham Estate taken by Shrubsole in 1879. F39

Photograph taken by Shrubsole in 1897 on the Ketteringham Estate at the garden wall near Bradbrook's house. L to R: Joe Bassingthwaite, Jon Emms, Frederick Cooper, William Bassingthwaite, Leo Bradbrook, Celia Bradbrook, J W Bradbrook. F40

Photograph taken by Shrubsole in 1898 of the Ribbon Walk leading to the west aspect of Ketteringham Hall. F41

Photograph taken by Shrubsole in 1897 on the Ketteringham Estate. Ketteringham Church. F42

2004, he states that the earliest photograph by Nokes in his collection is a wedding group dated 1891. Perhaps it was in this year that he became a master photographer in his own right.

His mother, Thirza, worked in order to look after Tom and May and in 1891 she is described as a nurse. The family say that she was an unqualified midwife being paid for attending local births, her personal experience being put to good use. In 1891 William Nokes was living at 5 Victoria Street on his own means. He was described as single. Tom and May did not see William or the children of the marriage because of the separation.

Tom married Ellen Mary Merry at Catton Church on 15 April 1895. Her parents, Alfred and Elizabeth Merry, lived in Magpie Road. Ellen was one of a large family and was a tailoress. There is a lovely photograph of her standing in a garden full of foliage wearing what was probably the very latest fashion – hat, and a high-necked blouse under a beautiful dress. The bodice has very wide lapels and the sleeves above the elbow are very full, tapering to a fitted sleeve over the forearm, with a light band at the cuff. Her skirt is full and she is wearing gloves.

(Left) Front of 9 Chester Street with 3 soldiers temporarily billeted there in WWI; all three were killed. F09

(Right) 9 Chester Street in 2010. F10

Portrait of Edward Nokes probably taken at 9 Chester Street. F11

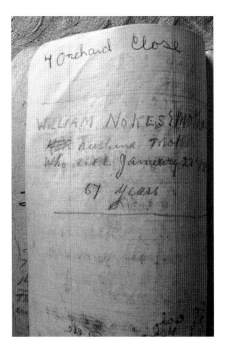

Tom and Ellen moved into 9 Chester Street directly after their marriage. It is a modest terrace house with three rooms on the ground floor and three on the first floor. The garden is very narrow, only about 12 feet wide, the same width as the house. Chester Street lies between York Street and Gloucester Street; it is pleasant, short and built on a slope. The area today is one of the most densely populated of Norwich but this was not so in the early twentieth century as there were overcrowded slums in the city centre. As with most terraces there are passages at intervals between the houses to give access to the back yards or gardens. Everyone would have known their neighbours, used the local shops, walked or cycled everywhere. Their occupations would have been as varied as was the choice of pubs after work. As the children were born and the family grew they would have had friends and good community support.

The Nokes Notebook

There is a small scruffy soft-backed cash book which Tom had for many years. The first legible entry is 'William Nokes – Mother's husband died 22nd January 1893, 67 years.' Then follow the dates of birth of all his family. He records when and where he married and the date of Ellen's death, stating that they were married for 37 years and lived at 9 Chester Street for that time. The next entry records his son, Reginald's, short army career and the dates when various members of the family died.

The information in the notebook then becomes random and more mundane. A list of names and addresses, a short list of decorating jobs recording his

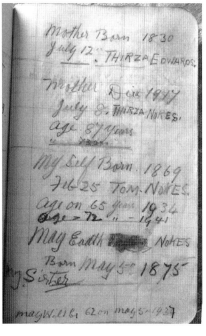

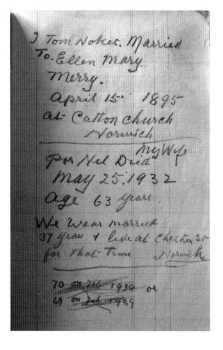

*Portrait of Florence with
picture book probably taken at
9 Chester Street.* F13

*Opposite page: (From left)
Tom's notebook 01. 'William
Nokes (Mother's husband)
who died Jan 22nd 1893, 67
years.' This has been added to
show that Tom knew that he
was illegitimate.* F51

*Tom's notebook 02. This page
gives Tom's date of birth.
Three short articles written
about Tom have given his
birth date as 1872.* F52

Tom's notebook 03. F53

employer, the dates he worked and the payment he received. This is followed by bus and tram numbers for various journeys in London and the name and address of a chemist in London where bronchial lozenges could be purchased, and a doctor's name and address in Clapham. There is a simple record of two bank accounts for himself and Florence between 1936 and 1939, the date he left Chester Street and the date he entered Doughty's Hospital. Finally, to add to the diversity of this notebook, there are a few names and addresses in another handwriting and some child has scribbled over two or three of the pages.

Portrait of Thirza holding May with Florence and Reginald probably taken at 9 Chester Street. F14

Portrait of Florence May and Reginald probably taken at 9 Chester Street. F15

From the notebook we learn that the eldest child, Florence, was born on 28 September 1895, followed by Edward on 23 February 1897 and Reginald on 27 February 1899. In the 1901 census Tom and Ellen and the three children are living at 9 Chester Street and he is a photographer working on his own account. The family would have been devastated when Edward died, aged 4, of diphtheria on 19 November 1901. There is a charming photograph of him on his own wearing a striped top with full sleeves and a collar covered with another large, lace, collar. He is holding a ball and staring intently at the camera. He appears again in a family group outside the house with Florence, baby Reginald and his mother and grandmother when both women are wearing dark, fashionable clothes and hats.

The youngest child, Thirza May (known as May), was born on 21 June 1902. During the years the children are growing up there are several enchanting photos of the whole family either inside or outside the house. Everyone is wearing beautiful clothes and looking happy and confident. It is known that Ellen made the children's clothes and probably her own as well. Sometimes Tom's mother, Thirza, is in the photo with various members of the family including her daughter, May.

In 1901 May, was living in London as a domestic servant in Stoke Newington. In 1915 she married Joseph Coltman at St Luke's Church, Battersea. Joseph was a mechanic in Government Service and they lived in Hillier Road, Battersea. Tom visited London to see them and occasionally they would visit Norwich. The notebook tells us of Tom's close relationship with his sister. It states, 'Joe died August 16th 1935, aged 58. For three weeks I stayed with May at London Monday August 19th until I come home Sept11th 1935. May come to Norwich November 9th stay with me until December 11th 1935.'

Nokes trade card. F16

Tom's Photography

Happily for local historians and postcard collectors Tom could not afford to rent a studio and so became an itinerant photographer, strapping his camera, tripod and leather bag containing glass negative plates to his bicycle. He cycled around Norwich and parts of Norfolk although his main activities were concentrated in south Norfolk villages. From the early 1890s to about 1904 he produced portraits, family groups, wedding groups, events, landscapes and the halls, manor houses and farmhouses of the landed gentry. He also specialised in animal photography taking portraits of championship horses, cattle and favourite dogs.

He built a shed in his garden for his developing but the family can remember this activity sometimes spilling out into the kitchen and front room. It is said that when the large number of glass plates could no longer be accommodated in his shed he buried them in the garden. The shed was also used as a studio for his paintings. His art work was a hobby. Perhaps after taking a photograph of his subject he then worked at his easel to produce the painting or maybe he painted his pictures on site. As well as building the shed he made a wooden trellis arch around the back door of the house which can be seen in several family photographs. The family also remembers that he carved a weathervane to be placed in the garden at his daughter's house.

In 1870 postcards were issued in Britain for the first time. These were plain cards which commercial companies used to acknowledge receipt of goods,

(Previous page) Portrait of Tom, Florence, Ellen, May and Reginald probably taken at 9 Chester Street. F17

Portrait of Tom, Reginald, Ellen, May and Florence in a colourful garden (it is too large for Chester Street). F18

confirm appointments and despatch price lists. At first the Post Office produced the cards but in 1872 firms were permitted to produce their own cards but they were not for sale to the public. In 1894 private postcards were produced for sale to the public and these quickly became very popular. Very soon the postcards were printed with a picture on one side. These pictures did not fill the whole surface and a short message could be written around the picture with the address only on the reverse side.

By the time of Edward VII's reign (1901–1910) these cards were extremely popular and in 1902 the Postmaster General authorised the divided back whereby the message and address were on the same side. Postcards of 1903-4 can still be found undivided, either because it took a long while for the old stock to be used up or they continued to print them in the old style. Norfolk was probably a little behind the times and Tom Nokes might have started producing postcards in 1903; nevertheless he certainly produced them in 1904. The postcards are of the highest quality as they are made from direct contact with the negative on to standard postcard photographic paper. They are printed with T Nokes and sometimes 9 Chester Street, Norwich. His name and address can be surrounded by a half circle or a full circle. The position on the card varies but is usually in the left- or right-hand bottom corner. Sometimes there was a title: he was not consistent.

Tom did not have a regular wage or salary nor did he have a good business sense and at times the family struggled, and it is believed that Ellen used her

(Previous page) Portrait of May, Florence and Reginald probably in the garden of 9 Chester Street. F19

Postcard advertising T Nokes and his photography, 1911. # F20

Trade card of T Nokes as photographer to the 1/4th Battalion of the Northamptonshire Regiment by Special Permit. F23

tailoring skills to supplement the family income. In about 1907 it is said that Thirza became ill and the family could not afford medical treatment. The nuns of the Convent of the Little Sisters of the Assumption, known as nursing sisters of the poor, came to the rescue and helped the family. It is thought that Thirza developed gangrene in her leg and eventually had to have the leg amputated. The family appreciated the nursing care of the nuns and Tom decided that all

Full length studio portrait of Tom during his middle years.
 # F24

Photograph of the back garden of 9 Chester Street showing part of Tom's shed, Reginald with a dog and May and Florence with skipping rope.
F25

the family should become Roman Catholic and the children should attend Willow Lane School. Florence was not pleased as she was enjoying her education at Bignold School. Interestingly, when Reginald filled in the form for the Army in 1917 he left his religion blank, so perhaps he was not happy with the family's conversion to Catholicism.

Photograph of Florence, Ellen and Tom in the back garden of 9 Chester Street. A rabbit is escaping Tom's clutches. F26

Tom's photographs were taken mainly outside and this meant there were many opportunities during the warmer months, but in the winter when it was cold and wet he must have found it difficult to earn money. He cycled fairly long distances with his equipment on his bicycle. It has been said that he used the train. This might have been so as he was getting older but unlikely in his younger days when the cost of the fare for himself and his bicycle would have been difficult to justify.

He travelled extensively in South Norfolk, in a large triangular area to the south and west of Norwich. Villages which he frequently photographed include Ashwellthorpe, Bracon Ash, Hethersett, Ketteringham, Thulbarton, Swardeston, Wreningham and Wymondham town. There are also photographs of Costessey and Panxworth, and postcards of Rockland St Mary and the halls

Photograph of Ellen in the background with Florence and May sitting in front of Tom's shed in the garden of 9 Chester street. F27

(Left) Half portrait of Florence probably taken at 9 Chester Street. F28

(Right) Portrait of Florence and Tom Jones. F29

of Blickling, Gunton, Oxnead and Tacolneston, and perhaps many others.

The range of subjects was huge. Portraits in a studio and outside, official events, weddings and funerals, group portraits, 1911 Coronation events and soldiers during the First World War. He photographed village lanes, harvest scenes, nurserymen, rural industries, delivery men with their carts, shop fronts with their owners and the occasional disaster. Halls, manors, farmhouses and churches were all recorded for posterity. He produced many kinds of trade cards,

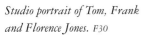

Studio portrait of Tom, Frank and Florence Jones. F30

multiple views, and Christmas cards to be sold in local shops. Even an Easter card has been found. With his artistic ability he was able to add decorative lettering and foliage to certain cards and he hand-tinted some of them. Tinting could be exacting work: the best fine brushes were made of sable. Tom tended to add fairly large blocks of colour and avoid colouring intricate details; the end result did not always enhance the photograph. He tinted several of his postcards of halls and manor houses and probably the owners enjoyed the more unique picture and paid accordingly. The number of tinted cards being produced overall at this time was very few.

Why did Tom decide to spend the majority of his time in the villages and at Wymondham when the opportunities in Norwich were numerous and varied without too much travelling? There may be several answers to this question. Shrubsoles gave him an introduction to some of the landed gentry and there was no competition from professional photographers in the village. There were several photographers in Norwich and Wymondham. Villagers spent most of their time outside whereas some of the workforce in Norwich worked in buildings and factories where entry would have been impossible. He was an individual and became well-known in the villages and was probably admired for his technical skills, his occupation being very different from those of the rural community. Tom did a little work in Norwich but he would have gone about his business mainly unnoticed in a city with many professional, business

Photograph of the wedding of May and Frederick Hornsby July 1926 (the original is hand-coloured, probably by Tom). On the left is Tom Jones, in the centre Tom Nokes and on the right Phyllis Hornsby. F31

May and Frederick July 1926. F32

Buckingham's shop, Hethersett (not a Nokes card). Walter Buckingham ran the Post Office and stores for over fifty years. He was a dapper little man, immaculately dressed in black jacket and striped trousers. It was a joke in the village that his fastidiousness did not include his shop as it appeared that the tumblers and jugs on his shelves had not been moved or dusted during his occupancy. His wife is standing in the doorway and it is said she sometimes intimidated the customers. F54

Tom Nokes with his brother-in-law, Joseph Coltman, probably in a London Park.
F34

and trades people. Perhaps Tom simply preferred the rural way of life in contrast to his own urban environment.

Tom was a sociable person and was a regular visitor to the local pubs where he made friends and met clients. He became involved in the life of the villages and particularly liked a game of bowls. He made himself known to the postmasters and storekeepers and received commissions from them. He produced postcards for Buckinghams of Hethersett, Middletons and Cracknells of Mulbarton, and Watlings of Bracon Ash. He recorded many village scenes over the years and knew that if he photographed a large group of people he was sure to sell a large number of postcards. It is fortunate that his artistry as a photographer sometimes overrode his business acumen and he would capture one or two people in an idyllic setting.

He would sometimes be invited for a drink when he delivered his postcards of manors, farmhouses or horses and prize cattle to the gentry or farmers. He was too proud to eat his sandwiches whilst drinking and would arrive home a little the worse for wear. He would take his postcards of the villagers at work or play to the pub to meet his clients for payment and perhaps when business was done they enjoyed a drink together. Occasionally his clients were unable to pay and gave him a ham or other items of food instead. With a small amount of money or only a ham Ellen had no way of paying all the bills, resulting in hardship for the family.

The First World War

With the start of World War I the opportunities for photographic work increased. Tom took portraits of soldiers about to go to war or on leave, proudly

(Left) Studio portrait of Tom and his sister, May Coltman, taken in later life. F35

(Right) Family photograph taken in the back garden of 105 George Borrow Road, 1930. Back row: Joseph Coltman, Tom, Frederick Hornsby. In the middle Florence Jones, May Coltman, and, in the front, Tom's grandsons, Frank Jones and Jack Hornsby. F36

wearing their uniforms. Sometimes these portraits included a wife or a small infant. Very sadly many of these men were never to return home again so that their last portraits taken by Tom were treasured by their families. There is a photo of three soldiers standing in front of 9 Chester Street where they were billeted for a short while: all three were killed.

In November 1914 the Essex Regiment was billeted for five months in Wymondham. Tom took a series of photographs of their activities in uniform and when off duty. From one such picture he created a Christmas greeting card with the men playing cards. This would have been eagerly bought by everyone on the card to send to their families at Christmas time. He obtained a special permit as photographer to the 1/4th Battalion of the Northamptonshire Regiment when billeted in Norwich from April to May 1915.

Tom also produced a card to advertise this work showing a head-and-shoulders portrait of himself appearing from the smoke of his pipe – Tom the Genie! He probably smoked a pipe all his adult life: he appears with his pipe in many photographs.

In October 1916 Reginald had a medical for the army and on 19 February 1917 he joined the army reserve. On 26 March 1917 he was enlisted in the 12th East Surrey Regiment. The following day he was sent to St Albans. He had leave in August and returned on 19 August 1917. On September 8th he was posted to Colchester. He had 6 days leave in January 1918 and was on leave again in Norwich from 15 March until 31 March. In April 1918 he joined the 1/21st London Regiment (First Surrey Rifles) and left for France. He was killed in action on 12 June 1918. Reginald's grave and memorial are in Contay British Cemetery in France.

The news of his death must have been overwhelming for the family. The heartache of losing their surviving son and brother, the pain being all the more poignant as years before they had to cope with Edward's death, albeit in very different circumstances. Thirza, his grand-mother, had died the previous year and was spared the family grief. She had died in the parish of St Thomas, most probably in the Infirmary on Bowthorpe Road, later to become the West Norwich Hospital, and she is buried in Earlham Cemetery in the Catholic section

Tom in later life. Location unknown. F37

Towards the end of 1918 Florence married Tom Jones. At first they lived in rented rooms and then moved to a terraced house not far from Cushions the timber merchant. John Wheatley, who was Minister for Health in the 1924 Labour Government, introduced the Wheatley Subsidy to encourage house building and private ownership. Florence and Tom, who now had a young son, took advantage of this, as did May after marrying Frederick Hornsby. They had 103 and 105 George Borrow Road built, a pair of pleasant semi-detached houses off Colman Road. Apparently No 105 was rented out for a short time and both families lived at 103. This arrangement did not last long and May and Frederick moved into 105.

The sisters had a close relationship and the arrangement would have suited everyone, with the families in close proximity whilst being independent. In a short while this was all to change as Tom and Florence moved to 3 Allen's Lane,

*Studio portrait of Reginald in
the uniform of the East Surrey
Regiment in WWI.* F21

Full length studio portrait of Reginald in WWI. F22

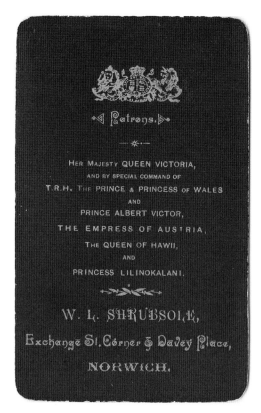

Sprowston so that Tom could be nearer his work. May continued to live at 105 for the rest of her life. The daughters sometimes had the help of their father in their gardens. He even cycled to Sprowston to help in the garden during the Second World War.

Change of Career

About 1926 Tom gave up his photographic career. Britain was in the depths of a post-war economic depression and there was a General Strike in that year. Farm workers' wages had been reduced and after the strike ended many farmers did not re-employ all their labourers. There was much hardship in the villages with a knock-on effect for village shopkeepers, bakers, butchers and blacksmiths etc. Spare money to spend on photographs did not exist. For the more affluent farmers and landowners cameras were becoming cheaper and they were probably taking their own photographs if required.

Tom records in his notebook that he did a painting a decorating job starting on 26 July 1925 for Mr Nobbs of Great Yarmouth. Other jobs started on 12 May 1926 for Mr Taylor of Cringleford, and on 30 March 1927 for Pearson & Son. There is a photo of him taken with members of staff while he was decorating a country house in June 1926. For two to three years he ran his

Photograph taken in 1926 of Tom as a decorator, with three servants at a country house. F33

Oil painting by Tom Nokes of Costessey Bridge, Norwich in 1910. F43

Oil painting by Tom Nokes, location unknown. F44

photographic business and decorating jobs side by side. From about 1927 he spent the rest of his working life as a painter and decorator.

Ellen died in 1932. Her illness was relatively short and medical help was not initially sought as it was too expensive. When she did seek help from the medical profession her illness was advanced; it may have been a form of cancer. Tom cared for her as best he could but she died on 25 May 1932 and is buried in Earlham Cemetery.

A picture painted by Tom of Mulbarton Old Hall. Printed as a postcard and sold to Watlings Stores at Bracon Ash. **M** *F45*

14 Belvoir Street, Norwich in 2010, where Tom had lived in 1937 and 1938. F46

Tom records in his notebook that he started a decorating job for Mrs Wones of 14 Belvoir Street, Norwich on 20 June 1933. His last recorded job started on 31 October 1934 for J Holmes. He was sick from 23 November 1934 to 4 January 1935 and he continued to live at Chester Street until 9 December 1936. The reason for leaving is not known but perhaps by this time he had ceased painting and decorating – he was now 67 – and he found it impossible to pay the rent from his pension.

In the register of electors for 1937 and 1938 Tom is at 14 Belvoir Street with Florence Wones as the occupier. Her address in Tom's notebook appears on the same page as three brothers-in-law and one other, unknown, person. Before she married she was a tailoress and it is possible that she was a friend of Tom's wife, Ellen, and a close friend of theirs during their marriage.

The family recalls that he visited his widowed sister in London on several occasions, and the notebook records quite a lengthy visit in 1937. 'Mrs Wones and Florrie (his daughter) come (sic) to London Tuesday May 11th 1937. Mrs Wones left May 20th, Florrie and myself left May 25th 1937.' It is probable that Mrs Wones and Florrie arrived on 11 May to be with Tom and his sister, May, so that they could all enjoy the Coronation of George VI on 12 May 1937 in London.

On 2 March 1937 Frederick Hornsby died at the age of 36 and May was left to bring up two small children on her own. With no mother to support her and a father preoccupied with looking after himself, life must have been very difficult. In order to provide an income for the family she took in paying guests. In the Register of Electors for 1939 Tom is residing at 105 George Borrow Road with his daughter May Hornsby. Apparently he arrived pushing a handcart which contained all his possessions. He had finished work and had no money. Among the items on his hand cart were many of his glass negatives. These were stored in a shed in the garden. When the family wanted to replace the shed with a garage in the 1950s some of the plates were thrown away while others were used as rubble for the foundations. No surviving plates have been found. Tom was unable to contribute to the family's finances and May needed both spare rooms for the paying guests so he only stayed a short time. He may have spent several brief visits with May and her two children over the next two years until he entered Doughty's Hospital on 23 August 1941, living at cottage No.26.

The hospital was founded by William Doughty in 1677 to accommodate 24 poor aged-men and 8 poor aged-women, each of whom was to have an allowance of 2 shillings every Saturday to buy food, to be provided with coal and a coat or gown of purple cloth. When Tom entered it was for poor elderly persons of good character. In 1934 there had been a complete relaxation about the number of each sex. A stipend for food and clothes was given weekly to those with a small pension, or no pension at all. Coal was provided. The accommodation was a bedsitting room with a cooking range and communal bathroom and toilets. There was a central reading room with a wireless, a laundry and nursing service.

In 1941 a nurse was congratulated on her prompt action in dealing with an incendiary bomb which fell on the green at Doughty's. In another raid the reading room was destroyed by incendiaries, windows were blown out and a

Doughty's Hospital 2010, showing flat No.13 bottom right, originally cottage No.26, where Tom lived. All cottages have been redesigned into comfortable flats. F50

cottage roof fell in. The Trustees, when visiting at this time, remarked in the visitors' book that it must be a consolation of old age for residents to take matters as they arise and to quickly readjust themselves to new conditions.

Tom's notebook records that on 28 August 1941 he received 15 shillings for boots. He had a new suit on 4 April 1942 and received another 15 shillings for boots in April 1943. Tom sometimes helped with the gardening and this was no doubt appreciated at Doughty's when so many men were away fighting in the war. This suggests that when he entered the hospital he was still fairly fit and active. But over the following two years his health deteriorated and Tom died on 30 December 1943 aged 73. The cause of death was given as senile decay and bronchitis. Tom and Ellen are buried in the same grave in Earlham Cemetery but there is no trace of a headstone.

The winning combination of Tom and Ellen's photographic and dressmaking skills produced portraits of the family which captivate the observer. They have created a fantasy of prosperous, genteel living far removed from the reality of their everyday lives. It would have taken time and effort to dress the children in their best clothes and get them to pose naturally in front of the camera, perhaps over time they did it instinctively. Future generations of the family have inherited a wonderful collection of photographs which has never been seen by the public until now.

Without the confines of a studio Tom was able to give full rein to his photographic talents which were never fully recognised in his lifetime. He had a natural gift for composition and was a master at capturing the sunlight. He has left an amazing legacy of evocative rural scenes, busy urban life, artistically arranged groups of people and soldiers during World War I. Through his images we have a visual record of peoples' occupations and industries, the type of clothes they wore, and the tools and equipment they used.

The people Tom photographed often had difficult lives equal to his own. He earned little money, bringing hardship to his family and during his life there were periods of great sadness. His postcards are avidly collected and he would be amazed at the prices they fetch today. The foresight of these collectors has secured a very valuable visual record of life in Norfolk at the beginning of the twentieth century for future generations.

The Photographs

Cabinet portrait of a young lady about 1895 wearing a dress, with very full sleeves from the shoulder to the elbow. A01

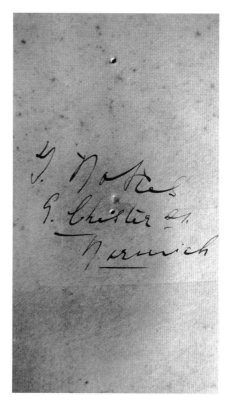

Reverse side of the photograph. A01r

A group of gypsies in a village with a cart, two traditional caravans, horses, goats, a pig and chickens. A lovely decoration on top of the central van with VR and a crown denotes Queen Victoria's Diamond Jubilee. # A02

Portrait of a couple in their garden, probably early twentieth century. The wife is wearing a large lace collar. A03

A school photograph taken c.1898 Nearly all the children are holding their hands behind their backs. A04

A more informal school photograph probably taken about the turn of the century. One or two of the boys have lace collars. A05

A wedding photograph taken in a back garden, in front of a garden shed (the foliage to the right could include rhubarb). Taken in the 1920s. A06

A wedding group taken in front of a cottage on Christmas Day 1913. It was not uncommon for couples to get married on Christmas Day or Boxing Day when the workers had two days off. Obviously Tom was working that day! A09

A portrait of a couple in front of their house, with two cats drinking milk in the foreground, taken during the Edwardian era. A10

Reverse of A10. If Tom didn't sign a photograph he stamped it on the back. A10r

Village photograph for the 1902 Coronation. A11

Stamp on reverse of A11. A11r

Village photograph for the 1911 Coronation. A12

Mr Price's bakery was in Starling Road, Norwich. The picture shows two bread carts with a motorised bread van in the centre. Taken from Magpie Road in the 1920s. A13

Billy Poll of the Lizard (outlying common land of Wymondham), shearing a sheep. A14 #, A15 and A16

Private Cecil Edward Beckett RE of East Carleton with his wife and child. He died of wounds in France in August 1916. A17

A wonderful village wedding group in South Norfolk, bathed in sunlight. A18

Another South Norfolk wedding group. A19

Old and new transport juxtaposed, circa 1910. The car belonged to George Peele of Stanfield Hall Farm, Wymondham. He is sitting at the front right. A20

J G Peele's turkeys at Stanfield Hall Farm, Wymondham. Rough-plucked turkeys hang in a shed.. Could the figure in the background be a policeman? A21

Postcards by location

A family group outside a cottage, probably grandparents with daughter and grandchild. Grandmother is carrying the washing. Ashwellthorpe 01

Central Stores in Ashwellthorpe with four villagers and a dog. The owner is standing outside the door. Ashwellthorpe 02

The blacksmith of Ashwellthorpe posing with two finished wheels and with the wheel-less cart in the background. Ashwellthorpe 03

Wood Farm, Ashwellthorpe. A boy posing with a bucket. It could be Tom's bicycle in the right hand corner with his bag for negatives.
Ashwellthorpe 04

New Road, Ashwellthorpe with an agricultural horse and cart on the right and a delivery cart with villagers in the centre. Ashwellthorpe 05

Blickling Hall, near Aylsham. At times Tom travelled quite a distance to take a photograph. Blickling 01

Dutchmen raising sugar beet, 1907. These men travelled to Norfolk from the Continent as farm labourers early in the year and stayed until after the sugar beet had been lifted in the winter. # *Bracon Ash 01*

Wartime Harvest, possibly late summer 1915. A traction engine working on Home Farm, Bracon Ash in the field behind the Village Hall with Archie Feltham (on binder); Lenny Eagle (white hat); Bob Loveday (on traction engine). The Contractor is G J Desborough of Wattlefield, near Wymondham (who appears in the 1916 Directory). The engine is a Wallis Patent, registration AP527. Soldiers were sent to help with the harvest in World War I. **M** *Bracon Ash 02*

Easter Card from Bracon Ash. Montage with a baby breaking out of the egg combined with a picture of a chicken. Bracon Ash 03

Bracon Ash and Hethel School, Bird and Tree team winners of the County Shield 1923. Each child has been given a medal and a book titled Tales About Trees *published by the Religious Tract Society.* Bracon Ash 04

Fred Loveday. Rifleman in the 10th Battalion of the Rifle Brigade. Killed in action in France December 1916. Bracon Ash 06

Bracon Ash harness shop, also a place to get boots and shoes repaired. Bracon Ash 07

Watlings shop, Bracon Ash – L>R: Billy Canham; Mr A Watling; Mac Watling, 1927. Bracon Ash 10

The Street with ladies and a dog standing in road (saddler's shop behind). A man leans against milepost sporting feathers in his hat – possibly Mike Mallet? Bracon Ash 12

Children on the green at the corner of Norwich Road and Hawkes Lane (a card posted to Miss Gladys Watling at Soham in 1904 'from Sydney'). The girl in the centre with long hair, holding the bike, is Gladys Watling. Bracon Ash 13

Hawkes Lane, Bracon Ash, from Norwich Road with families posing for Tom. Bracon Ash 15

Harvest field near the church, probably at refreshment time with the women and children. Bracon Ash 16

Bracon Ash Cricket Club, winners of the Tas Valley Cup 1909. Bracon Ash 17

Brick houses with five men outside, a card posted in 1910 to Master L Watling at Burnham Market – 'Love from Mama'. On far right is 'Bowler Scarf' the road sweeper. Bracon Ash 18

Hay crop on Mergate Farm, Bracon Ash. Drink is being dispensed on the cart. # Bracon Ash 19

Harvest field with man with gun and dog, labelled: M Thompson (gamekeeper); Fred Pottle (on binder); Loftus Watling (on horse); A H Watling (with cane and dog), taken about 1912. Bracon Ash 20

After the shoot, outside a barn near 'Woodlands'. Bracon Ash 21

Raspberry picking on Arthur Middleton's farm, Bracon Ash (before 1920). The fruit was sold to a jam maker in Norwich. Back row, L-R: Mrs Randell; E Middleton (holding baby); Mrs Smith; Charlie Middleton; Mrs Middleton (holding child?); Mrs Loveday {+ 1 ?}. Front row (seated): Rosie Stackard; Fred Loveday; Mrs Martin; Mrs Fred Stubbings. Bracon Ash 22

Raspberry picking on Arthur Middleton's farm, Bracon Ash (before 1920). The fruit was sold to a jam maker in Norwich. Charlie Middleton (far left, with child); Mrs Randall (holding basket); ? & Fred Loveday (standing at back); ? & E Middleton (with child at front); toward back right: Mrs Smith; Mrs Martin?; Rosie Stackard; Mrs Loveday (far right) Bracon Ash 23

The Peel Family. *Bracon Ash 24 – 32*

Peel baby. Bracon Ash 24

Peel girl in meadow. Bracon Ash 25

Peel mother & daughter. Bracon Ash 26

Peel mother & daughter a few years later. Bracon Ash 27

Walter Peel in WW1. Bracon Ash 28

Eliza Betts, grandmother of Ruby Peel. Bracon Ash 31

Family of four. Bracon Ash 30

Same family of four taken a few years later. Bracon Ash 29

Family group with dog — best lace collars for the boys. Bracon Ash 32

Women and children: L-R Blanche Mackerel; Willie Mackerel; Mrs Bright with Phyllis; Alice Mackerel; Mabel Mackerel. Bracon Ash 34

Wedding group – the Stackard and Dye families. Bracon Ash 35

Wedding couple (as in group, above), Percy Stackard and Rosie Annie Dye. Bracon Ash 36

*Frank & Mary Ellis on their
wedding day during WW1.*
Bracon Ash 37

Tom & Lily Bright with baby and Phyllis standing on chair – the family lived in cottage off the green that had once been a pub. Bracon Ash 38

Winnie Feltham (née Bright) standing in a garden. Bracon Ash 39

Percy – photo dated 11 May 1913. Bracon Ash 40

Man in bowler hat.

Bracon Ash 41

Three women and boy. Bracon Ash 42

Baxter
grandparents
with three
grandchildren.
Bracon Ash 43

Three children at a cottage gate, Costessey. Tom has travelled to the west of the city. He also visited Costessey to paint the bridge. Costessey 01

A view of Rectory Road, East Carleton with figures. On the left is Walnut Tree Cottage with Letter Box Cottage beyond. East Carleton 02

Willam Emms, chrysanthemum grower. A plantation of roi des blanc, Oct. 1916? East Carleton 04

East Carleton Manor. A late Georgian house owned by the Steward family: they also owned Gowthorpe Manor in Swardeston. When Gowthorpe became their main residence East Carlton Manor was let and the tenant, Major Best, bought it in 1921. In 1923 the house was sold by auction to Philip Tindal-Carrill-Worsley. His widow leased the Manor during WWII to a furniture retailer and remover and after the war the house was demolished. East Carleton 05

East Carleton Lodge, the home of Lord Lindley. East Carleton 06

Funeral of Lord Lindley (1828–1921). Son of John Lindley, a famous botanist and horticulturalist, he studied law at University College, London. He was made a judge in 1875, became a Lord Justice of Appeal in 1881, Master of the Rolls in 1897, a Lord of Appeal in Ordinary (1900–1905) and was highly regarded. East Carleton 07

Floral tributes to Lord Lindley. East Carleton 08

Jimmy Lee (third from right) Wymondham bill poster, at the Black Horse, Flordon 1917. Flordon 01

FUNDENHALL MILL,

Post mill at Mill Farm in a derelict state. The mill had a round house and powered a pair of French burr stones. The mill was run by the Bunting family for many years and ceased working in 1906. Fundenhall 01

Payne's Farm with two men and a child. Baskets and wooden crates are stacked behind the man on the right. Fundenhall 02

Rose Cottage with family members outside. Fundenhall 03

Sunder's Farm in some disrepair with couple outside. Fundenhall 04

Pegg's Farm, Fundenhall. Fundenhall 05

Tom was obviously expected as all the ladies are posing in their best clothes. Fundenhall 06

Evocative river scene reminiscent of P H Emerson's 'Gathering Water Lillies' which appeared in the book P H Emerson: The Fight for Photography as a Fine Art. *Hapton 01*

British Legion, Tasburgh and District Branch, at Hempnall. Capt. A T M Berney Fickling, M C placing wreath. Hempnall 01

Potash Farm. Demolished to make way for the Engineering Department at Lotus Cars. Sir John Boileau bought Potash Farm in 1851 but because of the notorious murders there in 1848 he renamed it Hethel Wood Farm. At some time it reverted back to Potash Farm. Hethel 01

The Story of the Rush murders. Hethel 02

The Execution of James Blomfield Rush on the Norwich Castle Gallows Saturday, 21st April, 1849

In 1848 James Blomfield Rush was living at Potash Farm, near Stanfield Hall, Wymondham. To buy the farm Rush had ...

borrowed money from Isaac Jermy, the Recorder of Norwich, who lived at the Hall. When repayment became due Rush found himself in financial difficulties and asked Jermy to extend the term of the loan, but there was much ill feeling between the two men and Jermy refused. On November 28th 1848, two days before the mortgage expired, Jermy and his son were murdered at the Hall by an intruder. The crimes were committed at about half past eight that evening when Mr Jermy was shot dead in the front porch of the Hall. His son was killed when he went to investigate the shot. Mrs Jermy alarmed at the noise, ran out from the drawing room into the passage and met the maid Eliza Chastney. They both hurried to the hall where they saw the intruder coming out of the dining room. He levelled a gun at them and fired twice, shooting Mrs Jermy in the arm and Eliza in the thigh. He then escaped by the back door.

Rush was suspected of the crime and was duly brought to trial. He pleaded innocence but to no avail. His mistress, Emily Sandford, provided the most damning evidence, testifying to his absence from Potash Farm at the time of the murder. Thus he was condemned to die on the Norwich Castle Gallows. Saturday, April 21st. 1849 was the date set for the execution, and from early in the morning a great crowd gathered in front of the Castle to witness the event. St. Peter Mancroft church bell heralded the procession to the gallows. Mr Pimson the Gaoler and his turnkeys shook hands with Rush and after a short prayer Calcraft, the executioner adjusted the rope, the cap was pulled over his face, and a moment later "the unhappy man was launched into eternity".

Stanfield Hall, Wymondham. Designed by William Wilkins the Elder in 1792, it is surrounded by a moat. Its exterior was Tudorised in the 1830s for the Rev. George Preston. After the murders Staffordshire pottery souvenirs of Stanfield Hall, Potash Farm and the figures of James Rush and Emily Sandford became popular. # Hethel 03

Old May Tree, thought to be the oldest in East Anglia. In 1841 it was reckoned to be at least 500 years old with the trunk measuring 12 feet 1 inch in circumference and the branches spreading over an area of 31 square yards. Villagers can remember how May Day celebrations included a scramble to the thorn to count the number of props holding up the boughs. Today it is in the care of the Norfolk Wildlife Trust. Hethel 04

Hethel church and lane with traction engine. All Saints' Church is probably Norman with pinnacles and battlements added much later. The Branthwaite family converted the north chapel into a mausoleum and rebuilt the chancel about 1730. Hethel 05

Cantley Run, Hethersett with Meadow Farm Cottages in the background. Hethersett 01

Cottage Laundry,1905. The village women did the laundry for the more well-to-do, including people in Norwich. The man and boy are carrying wood to heat the coppers. Hethersett 02

Mill Road, Hethersett with men posing in foreground. **H** *Hethersett 04*

Hethersett Cricket Club, 1906. **H** *Hethersett 08*

Buckingham, artesian well engineer from Mattishall, at Hethersett. Hethersett 09

Hethersett Hall. This is a late Georgian mansion and has been linked with the Back family for many years. The first occupier was Thomas Back, a solicitor with strong links with Norwich, being Sheriff in 1802, Alderman in 1808 and Mayor in 1809. The Back family owned the Hall until 1924 when Edward Gladden bought it. It is now a residential home for the elderly. Hethersett 10

A wedding in Hethersett, 1913. Hethersett 11

Hethersett Girl Guides c 1924. **H** *Hethersett 12*

Tree struck by lightning, with cattle. Hethersett, 27 April 1909 (see also page 112). Hethersett 13

Hethersett Coronation Festivities 1911. # Hethersett 14

Hethersett Coronation festivities 1911. A parade of children surround a small brass band. Some of the girls are carrying parasols. George Blake in front. Hethersett 14a

H H Childs cycle shop in Hethersett c.1905. Hethersett 15

Melton Road, Hethersett. A couple with the woman holding a parasol stand in front of a delivery cart, possibly a baker? Early council houses on the left. 1912. **H** Hethersett 17

PTE. R.W. MAPES, 1ST NORFOLKS.

Private William Mapes became a hero when he returned to Hethersett, having escaped from a German prison camp. The school was given a half-day holiday and the pupils and teachers joined in the welcome home with flags and bunting. **H** *Hethersett 19*

Wheat dibbling at Hethersett 1910. A hole was made every 3 or 4 inches, closely followed by someone dropping in seed. This job could be done by the elderly or children, earning a few pence a day. # *Hethersett 20*

Samuel Marshall of Wymondham beside the Old Oak at Hethersett with his horse and cart, selling all sorts of hardware. Hethersett 21

Hethersett and Little Melton Brass Band, 1913. **H** *Hethersett 22*

Greeting from Hethersett with Hurn House in the background.. The house was built in 1894 for the Back family. **H** *Hethersett 23*

James 'Mouldy' Copeman, fish merchant and woodman, in front of the King's Head, Hethersett. # *Hethersett 24*

A view along Great Melton Road, Hethersett, with a small part of Buckingham's shop on the far right. *Hethersett 25*

INTERSTING WEDDING AT HETHERSETT,

An interesting wedding, Hethersett. The groom was Stephen Knapp, a notorious village character less than 5 feet in height. He had served several prison sentences in the old Norwich Castle prison ranging from poaching to various acts of indecency. For many years he lived in a garden shed. In middle age he married Emma who was no paragon of virtue but she was a clean and tidy housewife. Tom has photographed the happy couple as they returned from church on foot being showered with confetti. Hethersett 27

NORWICH ROAD HETHERSETT,

A group of villagers outside the Queen's Head, Norwich Road, Hethersett. 'Bosco' Hickling on the right and George Moore 3rd from right. Hethersett 28

Photograph of the Carter Family, Hethersett. Hethersett 29

Railway Bridge near Cantley Run, Hethersett with a hay cart. A strange subject to send as a Christmas greeting! Hethersett 30

Multi-view card of Hethersett. Hethersett 31

Wood Hall Hethersett. In 1841 the Rev. William Wayte Andrew, vicar of Ketteringham, bought the Hall and lived there for over 40 years. His difficult and troubled relationship with Sir John Boileau of Ketteringham Hall is recounted in the delightful book, Victorian Miniature, *by Owen Chadwick. In recent years the hall has been the residence of successive Vice-Chancellors of the University of East Anglia.* Hethersett 32

Children's pageant in Hethersett in 1924, featuring 'The Old Woman who Lived in a Shoe'. # *Hethersett 33*

Another children's pageant card from Hethersett. The pageant was held in the grounds of Wood Hall. **H** *Hethersett 34*

An artistic multiview card of Hethersett with flowers. Clockwise from top: Hethersett Hall, Interior of Church, outside the Queen's Head public house, St Remigius Church and Hethersett Alley. Hethersett 35

A lovely snowy scene, Norwich Road Hethersett. Winter scenes by Tom are scarce. Travelling along unmetalled roads and lanes in the snow would have been very difficult. This scene was taken about five miles from his home. Hethersett 36

A view looking along the street in Keswick with a policeman and three villagers in front of the Post Office. Keswick 01

Red Cross nurses and wounded soldiers at Keswick Hall. Seated extreme left is Mr Gurney of Keswick Hall. Keswick 02

First and reserve champion at the Norwich Spring Show held on the Keswick Hall estate. Mr Hudson lived at Beck Hall, Billingford. Keswick 03

A harvest scene, possibly on the Keswick Hall estate, with traction engine, threshing machine and bags of grain. **M** *Keswick 04*

A pageant performed by members of the Girls' Friendly Society, produced by Miss C Gurney of Keswick Hall. Keswick 05

Multiview of Ketteringham. Top row L–R Charlie Wright feeding swans, interior of Church, exterior of Church; Middle Row L–R. West view of the Hall, High Street, Ketteringham Hall and lake; Bottom Row L–R Ketteringham Hall, Church Cottage, Charlie Wright with swans. Ketteringham 01

Ketteringham Hall. A Tudor house bought by Sir John Boileau in 1836. He employed Thomas Allason in 1839–40 to reconstruct the Hall in the Gothic style. He employed Thomas Jeckyll to make minor alterations in 1852. The Boileaus sold the Hall in 1947 to the Duke of Westminster. Ketteringham 02

West view of Ketteringham Hall. Ketteringham 03

St Peter's Church, Ketteringham. Situated close to the Hall on a site dating from the Saxon period. The tower, which was rebuilt in 1609, is partially covered in ivy. The top of the tower was restored and embellished by Thomas Jeckyll in the 1870s. Ketteringham 04

Coronation tree planting. To the right of the tree Sir Maurice Boileau and his mother, Lady Lucy. To the left is sister Margaret and Raymond Boileau (Maurice's brother who became the 4th Baronet), with villagers. Ketteringham 05

107

Coronation celebration in front of barns at Home (sometimes called Hall) Farm, Ketteringham. Just after dinner on 5 July 1911.
Ketteringham 06

Wounded soldiers at Ketteringham Park. In the centre of the picture, 3rd row from front is Dr Margaret Boileau, sister of Sir Maurice. Sir Maurice 2nd row from front, second from left, and the Rev Richard Keppel Hart second row from front second right, with villagers and scouts.
Ketteringham 07

Highland cattle in front of Ketteringham Hall. The man in the foreground is George Layley Estate Steward. Ketteringham 08

Members of Ketteringham Mothers' Union 1909. Back row L–R Mrs Delph, Flora Delf, Mrs Groom, Mrs Wood, Mrs Loyd and Mrs Took.
Front row L–R. Mrs Dawson, Mrs Woodrow, Mrs Smart, Mrs Dermedy. Ketteringham 09

A Silens Messor mower on a lawn at Ketteringham Hall. The man holding the horse is one of the head gardener's sons, possibly Leo Bradbrook.
Ketteringham 10

Charles Wright feeding the swans with Ketteringham Hall in the background. Charles was employed in the stables on the Ketteringham estate.
Ketteringham 11

110

A shoot on the Ketteringham Estate. Keepers and brushers with dogs; several men are wearing buskins. Ketteringham 12

Keeper's hut in Smee Wood on the Ketteringham Estate, with keepers preparing food for the pheasants and chickens. A wonderful study of light and shade. Ketteringham 13

*Chickens on string, Ketteringham estate.
Sitting hens having early morning breakfast
(photograph joined in the middle). Each
chicken is attached to a stake by a string to
be fed away from from their boxes for
hygiene reasons and then returned to their
rightful box. The chickens are sitting on
pheasants eggs.* Ketteringham 14

*Oak tree struck by lightning in Smee Wood,
Ketteringham, 27 April 1909 (see also page
91).* Ketteringham 15

A. Farrow of Mattishall with his traction engine powering a circular saw on the Ketteringham Estate, cutting up timber. Ketteringham 16

A break for the workers cutting timber on the Ketteringham Estate with Charlie Wright standing on the cutting bench. Ketteringham 17

Family outside Wellgate, Low Street, Ketteringham. Ketteringham 18

The occupants of Apple Tree Cottage, Ketteringham, standing in their garden amongst the flowers. Ketteringham 19

George Layley, Estate Steward and family outside Park Lodge,
Ketteringham Estate. Ketteringham 20

Mr J W Bradbrook with sweet peas 8ft high. Ketteringham 21

115

Mr J W Bradbrook in the rose garden at Ketteringham Hall.
Ketteringham 22

Blanche and Celia Bradbrook. A tinted card depicting the rose garden at Ketteringham Hall. Ketteringham 23

116

(Left) *Lady Lucy Boileau, widow of Sir Francis, 2nd Baronet. She is standing beside the 'Lilies Cross' which came from 'The Lilies', a house near Aylesbury, which she inherited from her Nugent relatives.* Ketteringham 24

Sir Maurice Boileau, 3rd Baronet, son of Sir Francis and Lady Lucy.

Ketteringham 25

Gang of workmen at Kimberley Station. Kimberley 01

Trade Card for C J Frost's business, Mulbarton. Mulbarton 01

The bowling green behind the Tradesmen's Arms, Mulbarton. A Middleton Series card for the village postmaster. The pub closed in 1969 and was demolished soon afterwards. **M** *Mulbarton 02*

The village pond, Mulbarton, with cottages and church tower behind. Mulbarton 03

Snowy Christmas card with two children standing on the frozen village pond. Mulbarton 04

A Multiview of the village. Top Row L–R Mulbarton Bridge, the Hall and the Common. Middle Row L–R Dry Village pond, Mill and Mill House and Norwich Road. Bottom Row L–R Frozen Village Pond, interior of church and Church Cottages and Church Tower.
Mulbarton 05

A harvest scene with two women agricultural workers, WW I. They are voluntary paid agricultural workers identified by a dark armband. The horse is pulling a hay rake. **M** *Mulbarton 06*

Harvest scene with horse-drawn cart, WWI. It is believed that the people include Mr Potter, Mr and Mrs Tooke and Mr and Mrs Albert Rice. The women wearing dark armbands are voluntary paid agricultural workers. **M** *Mulbarton 07*

A family group. Mulbarton 08

Old church cottages. **M** *Mulbarton 10*

WW1 Volunteers, wearing dark armbands, pose for the camera as a group at the back of the World's End public house, 1916. Two of Tom's clients are depicted. Fred Middleton, Postmaster, is 5th from left on the back row and Charlie Cracknell, Mulbarton shop owner, is at the left of the middle row. **M** *Mulbarton 11*

Artistic multiview with flowers and berries, sold at A C Cracknell – Supply Stores. Clockwise from top left – frozen pond looking at the Church, the garden of 'Woodlands', 'Woodlands', Mulbarton Hall, the Mill House and the capped remains of the windmill. **M** *Mulbarton 12*

Soldiers demobilised from WW1 photographed at the back of the World's End public house, Mulbarton, July 1919. The title indicates men from Bracon Ash, Hethel and Swardeston. **M** *Mulbarton 13*

A day's bag from the shoot in the Mulbarton/Bracon Ash area, 1912. L–R: A Watling; R Thompson; F Swain; D Middleton; Waxer Cooper (rat-catcher); J Hammond; F Stubbings; -?-; -?-; -?-; A Feltham; P Stackard; W Devereaux & his sons, 'Podger' & Edgar. Mulbarton 14

The Bowling Green at the World's End public house, Mulbarton. Circa 1910. Mulbarton 15

Is this a posed photograph of Tom Nokes bowling across the green? Mulbarton 15a

Mulbarton Post Office with the mill in the background. **M** Mulbarton 16

Farmworkers at Mulbarton building a hayrick. late Mulbarton 17

Wounded in Norwich at the Convent of the Little Sisters. The Little Sisters had looked after Tom's mother some years earlier. # Norwich 01

The grave of Edith Cavell, 1865–1915, a Norfolk nurse from Swardeston. She cared for wounded soldiers in Belgium and assisted in their escape to Holland during World War I. For these actions she was executed by the Germans on 12 October 1915. Eventually her body was brought back to England, thousands of people escorting the hearse to her final burial place in Norwich Cathedral precinct in 1919. Norwich 02

Officers of the Church Lads Brigade 1st Batallion Norwich Regiment 1917. Norwich 03

A fancy dress party in Crowe Street Norwich. Norwich 04

Tom has travelled quite some distance away from his usual area, to Panxworth, about nine miles north-east of Norwich. Panxworth 01

The Hall at Stoke Holy Cross. Henry Birkbeck commissioned Anthony Salvin to design the hall which was completed in 1853. It was built in red brick with diapering in the Tudor style with many crow-stepped gables and large chimneys. When Henry died in 1895 it passed to a son, Geoffrey. His mother and elder brother moved to Poringland and Geoffrey followed several years later, leaving the hall empty. It failed to sell in the early 1930s and was let for a short time. Occasional events were held there but it was demolished in 1938–39. Stoke 01

A multiview card with flower decorations showing, clockwise from the left, the Infirmary for the poor, the Red House with wind generator, the new Church organ and the Dun Cow Public House. Swainsthorpe 01

The Red House, Swainsthorpe, with a wind generator in the garden. Swainsthorpe 02

Sir Alfred Munnings RA lived at Church Farm from 1907 to 1911. Polly, his aunt by marriage, owned Church Farm and Munnings rented four rooms in the farmhouse for £10 a year. Mr and Mrs Lodes lived in the kitchen end: Lodes was the farm's yard man and his wife managed the dairy. Mrs Lodes agreed to provide Munnings' meals, clean his room and do his washing for 15 shillings a week. At this time Munnings met a vagrant, nicknamed Shrimp, who worked with horses. He became Munnings' favourite model during his time at Swainsthorpe.
Swainsthorpe 03

Mother with her child in a pram with passing horse and cart at Swardeston. Probably taken during World War I as the person on the right is in uniform. Swardeston 01

A wonderful view of Swardeston Common. The fishmonger arriving with his horse and cart with a basket of fish for sale balanced on his head.
Swardeston 02

A group of villagers outside the Dog Inn, taken during World War I. Bullard & Sons was a Norwich brewery, trading from 1867, and taken over by Watneys in 1963. Swardeston 03

Women workers at Church Bros Nursery, Swardeston. Swardeston 04

Demobilised soldiers; one or two are still wearing their uniforms. Swardeston 05

Demobilised soldiers' dinner at Swardeston 1919. Swardeston 06

THE SPORTS OF DEMOBILISED SOLDIERS. AT SWARDESTON 1919.

Demobilised soldiers' sports at Swardeston 1919. Swardeston 07

SWARDESTON WAR MEMORIAL.

The war memorial at Swardeston. Edith Cavell's name appears at the top of the list of those who gave their lives. Swardeston 08

134

British Legion Church Parade. Tasburgh and District Branch. Sunday November 7th 1926. There is a small band, a man carrying a wreath and several men wearing medals. Tasburgh 01

A view of the devastation and destruction caused by the floodwaters of the River Tas in Tharston. Tharston 01

These two photographs show the August floods of 1912. Workmen clearing the debris. They arrived from Stratford the day following the flood.
Tharston 02 and 03

Rebuilding of Tharston Bridge September 22nd 1912. # *Tharston 04*

Wreningham Rovers Football Club 1914. Wreningham 01

Samuel Folwell, pork butcher from Leicester, at Hill Farm, Wreningham. Wreningham 02

Lady Berners of Ashwellthorpe Hall with her valet, Alfred Hirison, outside a cottage in Folgate Lane, Wreningham, 1913. Wreningham 03

The Lane family at the Woodlands in Wreningham. Wreningham 04

Norwich Road, Wreningham, looking south with the Chapel, founded in 1810. Wreningham 05

Norwich Road looking north, with two horses and carts. Wreningham 06

The war memorial at Wreningham. Wreningham 07

All Saints' Church, Wreningham. The C13th tower collapsed in 1852. When it was rebuilt the rest of the church was restored and a north transept added. Wreningham 08

Highfield, Wreningham. Wreningham 09

The Poplars, Wreningham. 1914. Wreningham 10

Children posing for Tom, Top Row, Wreningham. Wreningham 11

The Homestead, Wreningham. A car is a very rare sight in Tom's cards. Wreningham 12

Greetings from Wymondham. Wymondham Abbey, taken from Becketswell Road, with the railway crossing gates closed. Wymondham 01

The Green Dragon, Church Street, is the oldest public house in Wymondham. Built in the fifteenth century, it survived the fire of 1615. A wonderful timber-framed building with three former shop windows facing the street. Wymondham 02

Pople Street, Wymondham, with the Dove public house on the left – which closed in 1912 – and Standley's shop on the right. Wymondham 03

Soldiers of G Company, 4th Essex Regiment off duty. L to R H Firmin, S Hammond, D Smith, Charlie ?, with a lad in civilian clothes.
Wymondham 05

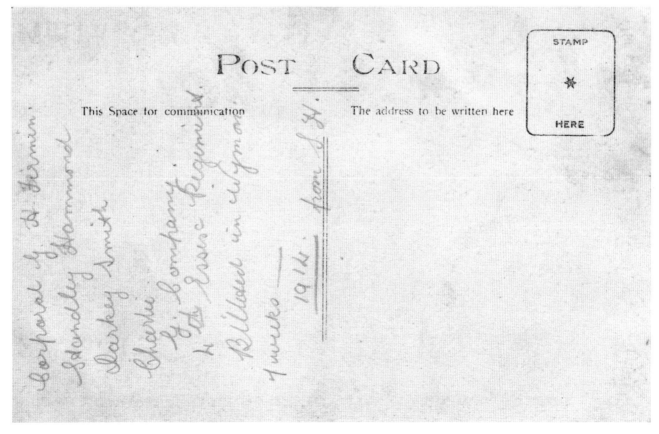

Reverse of Wymondham 05 *Wymondham 05r*

Soldiers of the 4th Essex Transport cleaning and polishing their saddles. Wymondham 06

Soldiers of the 4th Essex Regiment at Wymondham with horse and wagon, the soldier on the right with rifle and ammunition. Wymondham 08

Soldiers of the 4th Essex Regiment at Wymondham with sacks of hay and feed for the horses. Wymondham 09

Christmas Card 1914 showing Soldiers of C Company, 4th Essex Regiment, playing a relaxing game of cards. Wymondham 11

Two soldiers with army provisions. Wymondham 10

Official Portrait of 4th Essex Transport wearing ammunition belts. Wymondham 12

Dinner time for soldiers of D Company, 4th Essex Regiment. Wymondham 13

Two soldiers cooking up a meal. One of the ingredients is peeled tinned tomatoes. Wymondham 14

The war memorial at Town Green, Wymondham in the 1920's. ## Wymondham 15

The Funeral of Dr George Lowe in 1914.   He was a well-known local doctor in Wymondham. Wymondham 16

Wymondham Cricket Club.   Winners of the Saturday Junior Cup 1920. Wymondham 17

Wymondham Football Club, League Cup and Gold Medals Winners, 1921. Wymondham 18

Workers in the timber yard of the Briton Brush Company, Wymondham. It was formed in 1920, taking over from S D Page & Son. At the time brush factories were the major employers in the town. Wymondham 20

*Mr George Edwards, founder of the Eastern Counties Agricultural Labourers and Smallholders Union in 1908, with his agent, Mr Edwin
Gooch (left). Edwards won a 2118 majority in the South Norfolk by-election in 1920. Mr Gooch was elected President of the National
Union of Agricultural and Allied Workers in 1928 and held this position until his death in 1964. ## Wymondham 19*

Wymondham, Dereham and District Laundry Ltd at Norwich Road, Wymondham. What were piles of linen doing on the grass? Wymondham 21

The Wymondham sweep, 'Dusty' Goodings, with his donkey, cart and brushes. Photographed at Hethersett. Wymondham 22

Edward Warne, grocer and general dealer, outside his shop on the Lizard at Wymondham, 1910. ## *Wymondham 23*

Ernest and George Peele at Stanfield Hall Farm with seven tons of rough-plucked turkeys about to be transported to Wymondham Station.
Wymondham 24

Miscellaneous

Two farm labourers with three smartly-dressed ladies pitching the hay, posing for the camera.
Harvest 01 Z01

Village harvest scene building a haystack with the women and children bringing refreshments in their baskets. A young boy sits on the horse and another stands by a wheelbarrow. Harvest 02 Z02

Women, probably during World War I, carrying sheaves of corn to create stooks. A Land Girl is seen in uniform on the left and three other village women wear arm bands which were worn by paid female workers during the war. Harvest 03 Z03

A family with chickens. Z04

Father and son with two ponies. Z05

A family of four posing in front of chrysanthemums with a caption of 'A Jolly Christmas to You'. Z06

158

Maypole dancers. # Z07

Boys with dog – smartly dressed for the task of driving a flock of sheep along the lane. This was a common sight as animals were driven along the lanes and roads on market days. 1910. ## Z09

Woman with bicycle 1920s. Z08

Bibliography

Chadwick, Owen. *Victorian Miniature.* Hodder & Stoughton 1960.

Clarke, David. *The Country Houses of Norfolk – Part Two: The Lost Houses.* Geo Reeve 2008

Evans, Eric J and Richards, Jeffrey. *A Social History of Britain in Postcards.* Longman Group Ltd 1980

Goodman, Jean. *What a Go! The Life of Alfred Munnings.* Collins 1988

Hepworth, Philip. *Victorian and Edwardian Norfolk.* Portman Books 1987

Hethersett Society Publication. Heathersett Heritage 1999

Hethersett Society Research Group. *The Book of Hethersett.* Halsgrove 2002

Jewson, Charles. *Doughty's Hospital.* The Gildengate Press

McFadyen, Phillip. *Edith Cavell 1865 – 1915, A Norfolk Heroine.* 1983

Meeres, Frank. *Norfolk in the First World War.* Phillimore 2004.

Mortlock, D P and Roberts, C V. *The Popular Guide to Norfolk Churches 2: Norwich, Central and South Norfolk.* Acorn Editions, 1985

Munnings, Sir Alfred. *An Artist's Life.* Museum Press 1950

Newhall, Nancy. *P H Emerson. The Fight for Photography as a Fine Art.* Aperture 1975

Pevsner, Nikolaus and Wilson, Bill. *The Buildings of England. Norfolk 2: North-West and South.* Penguin Books 1999

Richardson, Robert. *Some Fell on Stony Ground.* Geo R Reeve 1978

Shaw, Michael. *All Our Yesteryears.* Alderman Press 1979

Soros, Susan Weber and Arbuthnott, Catherine. *Thomas Jeckyll, Architect and Designer 1827–1891.* Yale University Press.

Storey Neil. *Norfolk: A Photographic History 1860–1960.* Sutton Publishing 1996

Storey Neil. *Norfolk at Work.* Sutton Publishing 1997

Wright, Jill and David. *The Book of Mulbarton.* Halsgrove 2006

Yaxley, Philip. *Wymondham's Old Inns.* Wymondham Heritage Society 1991

Yaxley, Philip. *Wymondham and Attleborough in Old Photgraphs.* Sutton Publishing 1994